Town and Country Life

Peter Chrisp

LUCENT
BOOKS®

THOMSON
★
GALE

San Diego • Detroit • New York • San Francisco • Cleveland • New Haven, Conn. • Waterville, Maine • London • Munich

THOMSON

GALE

© 2004 by Hodder Wayland

Originally published by Hodder Wayland,
an imprint of Hodder Children's Books,
a division of Hodder Headline Limited
338 Euston Road, London NW1 3BH

For more information, contact
Lucent Books
27500 Drake Rd.
Farmington Hills, MI 48331-3535
Or you can visit our Internet site at http://www.gale.com

Design: Peta Morey
Commissioning Editor: Jane Tyler
Editor: Liz Gogerly
Picture Research: Shelley Noronha, Glass Onion Pictures
Consultant: Malcolm Barber

We are grateful to the following for permission to reproduce photographs:
AKG 35, 36; Art Archive 4, 5, 6, 7, 8, 9, 10 (top), 12, 17, 20, 22, 24, 25 (top and bottom), 26, 27, 28, 30, 32, 34, 37, 38, 40, 42, 44; Bodleian Library, UK 19 (top); Bridgeman Art Library/ British Library, London 11, 18, 21, 39/ Musee Condé, Chantilly, France 13, 14/ Musée des Beaux-Arts, Nîmes, France 23/ Palazzo Medici-Riccardi, Florence, Italy 29/ Archivio di Stato, Siena, Italy 41/ Universitatsbibliothek, Gottingen, Germany 42/ Banco Nacional Ultramarino, Portugal 45; British Library 10, 13 (bottom), 15, 19 (bottom), 31; Hodder Wayland Picture Library (title), 16; Topham Picturepoint 33.

Cover picture: © Archivo Iconografico/CORBIS

LIBRARY OF CONGRESS CATALOGING-IN-PUBLICATION DATA

Chrisp, Peter.
   Town and country life / by Peter Chrisp.
     p. cm. — (Medieval realms series)
Includes bibliographical references and index.
   ISBN 1-59018-536-6
   1. Cities and towns, Medieval—Juvenile literature. 2. Civilization, Medieval—Juvenile literature. 3. Villages—Europe—History—Juvenile literature. 4. Europe—Rural conditions—Juvenile literature. [1. Civilization, Medieval. 2. Middle Ages.] I. Title. II. Series: Medieval realms.

   D134.C47 2004
   940.1—dc22

                                2003024516

Printed in China

Contents

Europe in the Middle Ages   4

Landholders   6

Life on a Manor   8

The Peasant's Year   10

The Village Church   12

Lives of the Rich   14

Hunting   16

The Food of the Rich   18

Monks and Nuns   20

A Monk's Day   22

The Scriptorium   24

Pilgrimage   26

Town Life   28

Markets and Fairs   30

Guilds   32

The Hanseatic League   34

Famine and Plague   36

Peasants' Uprisings   38

The Cities of Italy   40

New Books   42

The End of the Middle Ages   44

Chronology   46

For Further Research   46

Glossary   47

Index   48

Europe in the Middle Ages

A THOUSAND YEARS AGO, Europe was very different from the place we know today. In the twenty-first century, there are more than 725 million Europeans, mostly living in towns and cities. In 1000, Europe was home to fewer than 40 million, more than nine-tenths of them living in the countryside as **peasants**, or poor farmers. Towns were few and far between, and one of their main roles was to provide a market for crops grown by the local peasants.

Three Orders

The Church taught that society was made up of three separate orders: nobles who fought, churchmen who prayed, and peasants who farmed for everyone else. In the eleventh century, a Frenchman, Gerard of Cambrai, wrote that this had always been that way: "From the beginning, mankind has been divided into three parts, among men of prayer, farmers, and men of war." In fact, there was a fourth group, which would play an increasingly important role as time went by— the **merchants** and **craftworkers**.

A medieval Italian town is surrounded by countryside, where crops are grown. In the distance executed criminals hang from a gallows.

In the centuries after 1000, hundreds of new towns were founded and land was cleared for farming. The population rose, reaching around 75 million in the 1300s. Then, in the 1340s, a terrible disease, the Black Death, arrived, which killed off one in three people. The frequent return of the plague throughout the fourteenth century meant it took until 1500 for the population to recover.

Following the Sun

Medieval people were more aware of the seasons than we are today. At different times of year, they did different work and ate different foods. They rose with the sun and went to bed at nightfall, so working days were much shorter in winter. Nights, even in towns, were much darker than now, for the only lighting was from fires, candles, and lamps holding tallow (animal fat).

Time was measured by the sun's daily movement across the sky, shown as a shadow on a **sundial**. A sundial, often found on the wall of a church, divided the day into twelve hours, which were longer or shorter depending on the time of year.

From the fourteenth century, the first mechanical clocks were built, which showed hours of fixed length, both in summer and winter. Yet the idea of organizing life according to the time shown on clocks, as we do today, would have baffled most medieval people.

Religion

Religion was of much greater importance than it is in modern Europe. Most Europeans were Christians, and members of the Church. They believed that they shared their world with invisible beings: angels, who were there to help and protect them; and devils, who wanted to harm them and lead them astray.

An English monk wrote a speech in which a merchant describes his life:

I am useful to the king … and to the wealthy and to all the people. I board my ship with my cargo and sail to lands overseas, and sell my goods, and buy precious things which aren't produced in this country. And in great danger on the sea I bring them back to you here; and sometimes I suffer shipwreck with the loss of all my goods, scarcely escaping with my life.

Aelfric, *Colloquy,* c. 1000

This woman is courted by a man playing a harp. The devils symbolize the temptation to sin.

5

Landholders

IN THE MIDDLE AGES, people were often said to hold land from a king or other lord, rather than to own it outright. The great lords, who held their lands directly from the king, were called his tenants-in-chief. For the right to their lands, they had to pay taxes and provide services, such as supplying the king with **knights** in wartime. In turn, the great lords allowed lesser lords, called sub-tenants, to hold lands for them in return for similar services and rents.

Landholdings were organized in units, known in England and France as manors. A manor could be a single village, or just part of a village. A lesser noble might hold just one manor, a village where he would also live, while a great lord could have hundreds, scattered across the country.

In exchange for the right to hold lands, a lord had to kneel in front of a king and make a vow, or solemn promise, to be his loyal servant.

Domesday Book

In 1066, the Normans under William the Conqueror (1066–1087) conquered England. William kept some lands for himself, and distributed the rest among his most powerful nobles. Twenty years later, he ordered a survey of his kingdom,

---

A typical *Domesday Book* entry describes the village of Wiston in Sussex:

Ralph holds Wiston from William…. There is land for eight ploughs. In the demesne are two ploughs. There are ten villans [serfs] and twenty-four bordars [smallholders] with five ploughs. There is a church, five slaves, seven acres of meadow, and woodland for thirty pigs. Before 1066, and now, worth twelve pounds.

to find out who held which manors, how much they owed him in taxes, and whether he could get any more from them.

William's officials traveled throughout the land asking questions, such as "Who holds the manor?" and "How many villagers are there?" Their findings were recorded in a huge book, later known as the ***Domesday Book***. Thanks to the *Domesday Book*, we have an amazingly detailed record of England in 1086–1087. It tells us that most of the land was held by 190 Norman barons, while a quarter of the whole kingdom was in the hands of just a dozen great lords.

Peasants

The *Domesday Book* names different classes of peasant, ranging from the free to those who were **slaves**. Most peasants belonged to a class in between, called villans in the *Domesday Book*, but better known as **serfs** or **villeins**. They were not free, though they had more rights than slaves. They could hold land and grow their own food, yet they were also expected to work on their lord's fields, called his **demesne**, and give him part of their produce as rent. The children of serfs grew up as serfs belonging to the same lord.

Some serfs were better farmers than others, and were able to grow more crops. These might pay rent in crops or money to their lord, instead of having to work on the demesne. Some could afford to hire other peasants to work for them, or to work for their lord on their behalf.

In June, peasants all over Europe had to cut grass with scythes to make hay.

Fines and Beatings

A serf could not marry, sell an ox, or leave the village without his lord's permission. Those who tried to run away, or disobeyed their lord, could be punished with fines and beatings. A thirteenth-century writer, Bartholomew the Englishman, described a serf as someone who "suffers many wrongs and is beaten with rods." Many lords saw their serfs as little more than animals. In legal documents such as wills, a serf's children were called his sequela (offspring), a word also used for a litter of piglets.

Life on a Manor

ACROSS EUROPE, there were many different types of manor. One common type in northern Europe was based on two or three large open fields. These were divided into strips, some part of the lord's demesne and others held by individual peasant families. Each strip was around 650 feet long, the distance that a team of oxen could pull a plow before needing to rest. This is the origin of the word furlong, meaning a **furrow** long. Each year, one field in turn was left **fallow**, so that the soil could recover its goodness, while the others were planted with crops, such as wheat or barley.

Beyond the fields, there was common land, which everybody had the right to use. This included pasture, where cows and sheep grazed, and a meadow, where grass was grown to make hay. Woodland supplied timber, firewood, and nuts and roots for pigs.

Manor Officials

Lords employed officials called **bailiffs** to collect their rents and make sure that the serfs did not try to cheat them. The day-to-day work was organized by the **reeve**, a type of farm manager. Unlike the bailiff, he was a serf. He was not paid, but did not have to pay rent or for other services. The reeve had to keep a close eye on the other serfs. Walter of Henley, author of a thirteenth-century farmer's handbook, wrote, "Let the reeve be all the time with the serfs in the lord's fields.... Serfs neglect their work and it is necessary to guard against their fraud."

In villages, peasants often had to work with their neighbors doing communal (group) work such as building fences.

Mills

Serfs were expected to grind their grain at their lord's mill, paying him a fee. This was an important source of income for a lord and serfs caught grinding their own grain, in **hand mills**, were heavily fined. Early medieval mills were powered by water. Then, in the late twelfth century people began to build windmills, an idea brought to Europe from the Middle East. Unlike watermills, which needed fast-flowing water, windmills could be built almost anywhere. They did not stop working when rivers dried up in summer or froze in winter.

Serfs harvest wheat under the eye of the lord's official, the reeve, who has the power to beat them with his stick.

Bailiffs and reeves had to report to a senior official, called a **steward**, who managed all the lord's manors for him. Every three or four weeks, the steward or lord held a court to sort out peasant arguments, to protect the lord's rights, and to punish wrongdoers. Serfs did not write books, so manor court records give us our best and most vivid source of information about their daily lives.

Serfs spent all their lives in the same village, alongside the same neighbors, all working together in the fields. Everybody knew everyone else's business and there were frequent quarrels between neighbors.

An English serf, Walter of the Moor, was caught stealing a fish from his lord's pond. At the manor court, he explained why he had done this:

I went the other evening ... and looked at the fish which were playing in the water, so beautiful and so bright, and for the great desire that I had for a tench I laid me down on the bank and just with my hands ... I caught that tench.... My dear wife had lain abed a right full month ... and she could never eat or drink anything to her liking, and for the great desire that she had to eat a tench I went to the bank of the pond to take just one tench.

The Court Baron, a record of manor court hearings

The Peasant's Year

MICHAELMAS, the festival of Saint Michael, on September 29, marked the end of one farming year and the beginning of the next. Once Michaelmas arrived, everybody knew that it was time to plow one of the fields, and plant a crop, such as wheat, scattering the seeds by hand. Then the field was harrowed—the soil was raked to cover the seeds. Meanwhile, children protected the seeds from birds, shooting stones at them from slings. If they managed to kill a bird, they would take it home for the cooking pot.

A peasant knocks down acorns to feed his pigs, while his wife spins wool into thread.

Long Hard Work

Martinmas (November 11) was the time when the older farm animals were killed. As there was no refrigeration the meat was then salted to preserve it. Through the winter months, the peasants cleaned out ditches, mended fences, and spread dung on the fields.

A horse pulls a harrow, a toothed frame used to cover the seeds with earth. Harrowing was done to protect the seeds from being eaten by birds, seen here being shot at by a man with a sling.

Pigs

Most peasants owned pigs which, unlike modern pigs, were small, dark, and hairy. A pig was the one animal that thrived through the winter, feeding in the woods on acorns and roots. As well as being a source of meat and black puddings, made from blood, pigs were used for tallow (fat) for lighting, leather, and bristles for brushes. A use was even found for their soft bones. These were boiled down to mush, which was fed to other pigs.

10

In August, the wheat was harvested. The height of the wheat in this picture is the sign of a good harvest.

In early spring, the remaining fields were plowed, and one was sown with a second crop, such as oats or barley. In June, peasants cut the grass in the meadow to make hay, which would feed the farm animals in winter. The number of animals they could keep alive through winter depended on the amount of hay gathered. After haymaking, the fields where the crops were growing had to be weeded. Peasants hated this work, which meant bending over for long hours tugging at thistles.

Harvest Celebrations

The busiest time of the year was the harvest, in August and September. Everybody worked hard from dawn to dusk, gathering the crops by hand, using sickles. To separate the grains from the chaff (husks and stalks), the crop had to be threshed (beaten). This was done with a flail—two pieces of wood joined together by a leather strap. The threshed crop was then winnowed—tossed in the air—so that the lighter chaff blew away.

Once the harvest was safely in, the peasants celebrated with a feast. Then it was Michaelmas once more, and the whole cycle of work began all over again. If the peasants were lucky, each year there was a good harvest. If they were unlucky, and the harvest was bad, they would have a hungry winter ahead of them.

Women's Work

Apart from working in the fields at harvesttime, peasant women watched over their children and looked after their gardens, where they grew vegetables and kept chickens. They also milked sheep and cows, made butter and cheese, and brewed ale. Every day, they cooked the family meal in a brass pot over the fire. This was usually pottage, a stew of grains, beans, vegetables, and sometimes a little meat, eaten with coarse bread. In any spare time, women spun and wove wool and flax, making clothes for their family.

The Village Church

THE CENTER OF PEASANT LIFE was the church, which was one of the few stone buildings in a village. Its walls were decorated with religious paintings, the only pictures that most peasants ever saw.

People were expected to give a **tithe**, or tenth part of their produce, to their priest, to feed and keep him. He was supposed to teach the villagers the Christian faith. However, many village priests were badly educated peasants themselves.

After Death

Medieval Christians believed that after death, they would go to another world, where they would be rewarded or punished for the lives they had led. The wicked would burn in hell for all time, while those who had lived holy lives would go to heaven, to be with God. Paintings in village churches often showed the terrible sufferings of the dead in hell, and the good climbing up to heaven.

Most Christians were not holy enough to go straight to heaven. So people believed that a third place existed, called **purgatory**. This was a place of suffering, like hell, but its purpose was to purge, or burn away, the dead person's faults, so that they would be worthy to go on to heaven.

Another belief was that Christ would one day come back to make a last judgment on all the living and the dead. Earth and purgatory would be emptied as everyone went either to heaven or to hell.

Mass

On Sundays and holy days, the villagers went to church to listen to the priest say a service called **Mass**, which was in Latin, a language that none of them understood. At that time, most Christians believed that during the service a piece of bread and

Blessings and Curses

Farmwork was full of risks. Bad weather, disease, and pests could destroy crops and kill animals. In this uncertain world, people often turned to the priest for help. He was thought to have the power to **bless** and to **curse**. Peasants brought their sick animals to him to bless, and they asked him to curse the pests that damaged their crops. The ringing of the church bells was also believed to drive away bad weather.

A familiar scene on church walls across Europe was the sufferings of the wicked, burning in hell.

a cup of wine turned into the body and blood of Jesus Christ. At the end of the service, the priest ate the bread and drank the wine. Eating Christ's body and drinking Christ's blood is called taking **Communion**.

Most peasants only took Communion once a year, on Easter Sunday. In order to be worthy to eat the holy bread, they first had to confess their **sins** to their priest. During the week of Shrove Tide (**confession** time), they had to tell him about all the bad things they had done in the previous year. He then gave them penances, such as saying prayers, to make amends to God.

Stages in Life

Ceremonies marked all the big stages in the peasants' lives. They brought their babies to be baptized. The priest poured holy water over the baby's head and made the sign of a cross. Couples were married by the priest in the church. He visited the dying, to hear their last confessions and to give them Communion. He held funeral services for the dead, who were buried in the churchyard in unmarked graves.

Because they visited the dying, priests were linked in many people's minds with death and bad luck. In the thirteenth century, Jacques de Vitry, a French churchman, complained, "In certain districts I have seen men when they meet priests immediately crossing themselves, saying that it is an evil omen (sign) to meet a priest."

A handbook for village priests suggested questions to ask a serf at confession time:

Let serfs be asked whether they have cheated by holding back their tithes, whether they have failed to show reverence (respectful awe) to their lords or have withheld their services, and whether they have made inroads on their neighbours' land with ploughs or cattle. Serfs often sin in this way: they will work hard in front of a man's face, but only feebly once his back is turned. If they are told off, they will murmur, and labour all the worse.

John de Burgo, *Pupilla Oculi*, 1385

Above: In church, worshippers kneel to be blessed by a priest, who sprinkles holy water on them, thought to drive away devils.

Left: A baby is baptized with holy water by a priest.

Lives of the Rich

THE LIVES OF THE RICH were very different from those of the peasants who worked to feed them. Yet they also lived in communities with little privacy, where everyone knew everyone else's business. Great lords had large households. At Berkeley Castle in England, Thomas Lord Berkeley (1245–1321) shared his home with over two hundred people, including his wife, children, knights, **men-at-arms**, squires (young men training to be knights), officials, and servants.

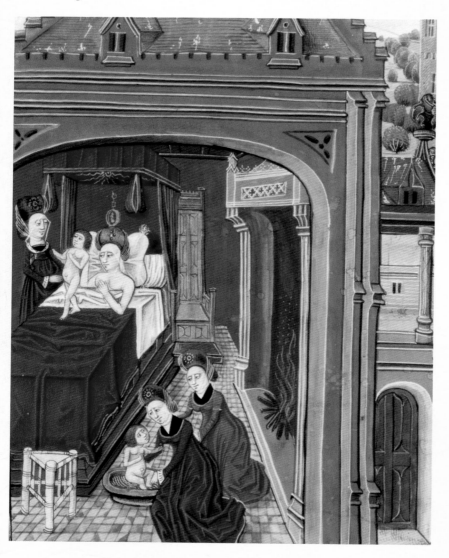

In this fifteenth-century illustration, midwives attend to the birth of a baby to a wealthy woman.

Marriage

In 1267, Thomas Berkeley married Joan Ferrers (*c.* 1248–1309), daughter of the Earl of Derby. The marriage, arranged by the couple's parents, was a business agreement between two great families. Joan brought with her an expensive **dowry**, lands given by her father. Her main role was now to have children, to produce an heir to keep the family going. Nobles wanted to have as many babies as possible, for it was common for children to die young. Between 1275 and 1283, Joan gave birth to seven children, which means that she was pregnant almost every year. Luckily for Joan, all her children survived to reach adulthood.

Castle Life

The most important official in Berkeley Castle was the **chamberlain**, who made sure that the castle was properly supplied with food and fuel, and that the servants did their work properly. There was also a family priest, who said Mass every morning in the castle chapel.

Berkeley Castle's biggest room is the Great Hall, which is 62 feet long, 32 feet wide, and 33 feet high. This was where the meals were served and where Lord Berkeley met his stewards and bailiffs, the managers of his lands. The walls were covered with colorful hangings of heavy cloth, which helped to keep out drafts. Although it had a large fireplace, the room's size meant that it was usually cold. Even indoors, the rich kept warm by dressing in heavy fur-lined robes.

Training for War

Lord Berkeley spent much of his life fighting, in wars against the French, Welsh, and Scots. As an old man of seventy-four, he was still going to war, against the Scots. Serving alongside him were his eldest son, Maurice, and two grandsons. The need to be skilled in warfare shaped the lives of noblemen. From an early age, Berkeley's sons were taught to ride a horse wearing armor, and to fight with a sword or lance. In peacetime they took part in tournaments—gatherings of knights to practice fighting skills. Events in a tournament included mock battles and jousts —single combats between two knights on horseback. Although tournaments were supposed to be sport, they could be very dangerous. In 1240, sixty men were killed during one German tournament.

Knights joust, watched by an audience, including ladies. One of the main aims of the contestants was to impress the ladies.

The French writer Jean de Froissart described a powerful blow struck by a knight, Sir Regnault de Roye, in a jousting match:

Sir Regnault hit him on the shield with such a firm, powerful thrust, delivered with so strong an arm—for he was one of the strongest and toughest jousters in France at that time, and also he was truly in love with a beautiful lady, and this contributed greatly to his success— that his lance pierced the left-hand side of the English knight's shield and went straight into his arm.

Jean de Froissart, *Chronicle*, 1390s

Hunting

THROUGHOUT THE MIDDLE AGES, much of Europe was covered by woodland, where wild animals, such as boar, deer, bears, and wolves could be found. Hunting these animals was the most popular pastime of European nobles. They chased after them on horseback with packs of hunting dogs. Once the dogs had cornered the prey, the nobles went in for the kill, armed with swords, spears, bows, and arrows.

This sport had two practical purposes: providing meat for the table, and practice in skills useful in war. Yet the nobles' main reason for hunting was their love of the excitement of the chase. In 1387, a French nobleman, Gaston Phoebus, Count of Foix, wrote, "All my life I have taken delight in three things: war, love and hunting."

Hunting Laws

To protect the supply of wild animals, kings made laws controlling hunting. In England, King William the Conqueror (1066–1087) declared that large areas of the country were royal forests—areas where only he was allowed to hunt. William

One of the most dangerous animals to hunt was the wild boar, with its sharp curved tusks. A French nobleman described the risks of boar hunting:

The boar kills with a single stroke, as one might with a knife. He is a fierce beast ... I have seen him strike a man and split him from knee to chest, so that he fell dead without a word ... he has often brought me to the ground, horse and man together, and killed my horse.

Count Gaston Phoebus of Foix, *Book of Hunting, c.* 1387

Noblemen ride after a stag, following their pack of hunting dogs.

A French painting from a fifteenth-century book on hunting shows men and women using hawks to catch ducks and herons.

employed hundreds of forest officials to make sure that nobody else hunted there. People who were caught killing deer were punished by being blinded.

European rulers gave rich nobles permission to have their own deer parks—areas of private woodland for hunting. These were surrounded by deep inner ditches and high outer banks and hedges, cleverly designed so that deer could jump into the park, but not escape again.

Birds of Prey

Men, women, and children hunted with trained birds of prey, which were flown after partridges, ducks, pigeons, and other birds. There were several types of hunting bird, which were believed to have different ranks, like people. The most beautiful and expensive was the white gyrfalcon, which came from Iceland and Scandinavia. The gyrfalcon was a bird prized by kings.

For nobles, the most popular bird was the peregrine falcon, valued for its speed and skill at catching prey. Pero Lopez, a Spanish nobleman, described the peregrine falcon as "the noblest and best of birds of prey, the lord and prince of hunting-birds."

The least prized bird was the kestrel, looked down on because it could only catch small birds, such as sparrows, and would even eat slugs and worms. Kestrels were said to be suitable for servants and children to hunt with.

Alfonso XI, king of Castile and Leon in Spain (1312–1330), wrote a book about hunting in which he explained why the sport was useful training for war:

A knight should always engage in anything to do with arms … and if he cannot do so in war, he should do so in activities which resemble war. And the chase is most similar to war…. One must be well horsed and well armed; one must be vigorous, and do without sleep … rise early … undergo heat and cold, and conceal one's fear.

Alfonso XI, *Book of Hunting, c.* 1330s

The Food of the Rich

NOBLES ROSE AT SUNRISE, perhaps breakfasting on a little bread and wine. By late morning, they were ready for dinner, the main meal of the day. Supper, a lighter meal, followed at dusk, or soon after.

Unlike their peasants, the rich ate vast amounts of meat. They thought of vegetables as food for the poor. The only limits on the amount of meat they could eat were those set by religion. The Church taught that people should give up meat and dairy products during the forty days before Easter, on Fridays and Saturdays, and on many **fast days**, on the eve of big religious festivals, such as Christmas. On these meatless days, nobles ate great quantities of fish.

An English poem lists the dishes in a meal in a castle on Christmas Eve, when meat was forbidden by the Church:

Several fine soups, seasoned in the best manner, and a double quantity of them ... and many different kinds of fish, some grilled on the embers, some boiled, some stewed and flavoured with spices, and all subtly sauced so as to please.

Author unknown, *Sir Gawain and the Green Knight*, fourteenth century

A group of musicians entertain the diners at a rich feast. The lord sits at his table at one end of the long hall.

Feasts

For Christmas Day, weddings, and other special occasions, the rich held great feasts in the halls of their castles. While the lord and his family sat behind a high table at one end of the room, the guests sat behind long narrow tables, which ran down the hall's sides. The fronts of the tables were used by servants, who brought the dishes and served the wine.

At the beginning of the feast, servants called ewerers carried bowls and jugs of scented water and towels to each guest, so that they could wash their hands before eating. This was because people ate with their fingers, and fellow diners did not like to see dirty fingers touching the food.

In the early Middle Ages, there was very little tableware. Instead of plates, people ate from flat slices of stale bread, called trenchers. They cut the meat with their own knives, which they carried in their belts. Forks did not come into general use until the late seventeenth century.

Cook Books

We know what was eaten at feasts thanks to medieval cook books. It was common to serve three huge courses, with around a dozen different dishes in each. There was no particular difference between each course, which might mix sweet dishes and meat or fish.

In 1397, King Richard II of England (1377–1399) held a feast, in which the first course included boars' heads, roasted swans, pike, and venison in a sweet spiced wheat porridge called frumenty. The second course had roasted cranes, pheasants, herons, peacocks, and rabbits. For the third course, there was spiced pork pudding, dried fruits, and eggs in an almond sauce, and pigeons, rabbits, quails, and larks, all roasted.

Above top: The large staff of a noble's kitchen, at work.

Bottom: Cooking meat over an open fire, on spits and in a cauldron, was hot work for the cooks.

Spices

The rich loved highly spiced food. Spices, including pepper, ginger, cinnamon, cloves, mace, and saffron, came from India and islands further east. On their long journey west, these were bought and sold by a series of merchants, who all raised their prices to make a profit. By the time they reached Europe, only the very richest people could afford them. So, serving heavily spiced dishes was a way of showing wealth and rank.

Monks and Nuns

MONKS AND NUNS were men and women who lived apart from the everyday world in religious communities. Each community, called a monastery or nunnery, was like a family, headed by an abbot (father) or abbess (mother). Becoming a monk or nun meant making a vow, or promise, to obey the abbot or abbess. Monks and nuns were forbidden to own personal property or to marry. They dressed alike, in plain robes, called habits.

Monks and nuns followed a strict rule, or set of instructions for daily life. The best-known rule was written in the sixth century by an Italian, Saint Benedict (*c.* 480–547). Saint Benedict declared: "Let nobody in the monastery follow his own heart's fancy." He wrote that a monk should be humble, always walking with "head bowed and his eyes towards the ground."

Until the twelfth century, monks were often recruited as children, offered to monasteries by their parents. Orderic Vitalis, born in England, described how he became a monk:

My weeping father, Odeler, gave me, a weeping child, to Rainald the monk, and never saw me again. A small boy did not dare to disobey his father ... and so I left my country, my parents, all my family and friends. At ten years old, I crossed the British Sea (Channel), and came, an exile, to Normandy, knowing no one, known to none.

Ecclesiastical History, c. 1140

This praying nun holds a set of beads, called a rosary, to remind herself of a set number of prayers.

The Work of God

The main purpose of monks and nuns was to offer group prayer. This took the form of the singing of the Psalms, a book of 150 Bible songs praising God. Once a week, the monks and nuns worked their way through all the Psalms, singing them at seven daily services and one in the middle of the night. This constant round of worship, called the Work of God, was thought to help everyone in the battle against the devil.

Monasteries

In Saint Benedict's time, monasteries were small, simple communities, in which the monks had to grow all the food they ate. Over time, monasteries became richer, thanks to gifts of land and money from kings and nobles. Abbots and abbesses became rich and powerful landowners, and most of the work was now done by peasants.

As their communities grew bigger, it became necessary for different monks and nuns to perform special roles. The almoner gave food and drink to the poor who begged at the gates. The cellarer organized the supply and storage of food and wine. The infirmarer was in charge of the infirmary, where the sick and the old monks were cared for.

Monasteries attracted traders, who set up shops to sell goods that the monks needed. In places such as St. Albans in England, towns grew up around the monasteries. The townspeople paid rents to the monks, who became even richer as a result.

Guesthouses

The bigger monasteries included guesthouses, which provided accommodation for travelers, especially kings and nobles. Medieval kings spent much of their time moving around the country in order to show their power to their people. They would stay in monasteries, where the monks would have to provide food, beds, and stabling for the horses. The guesthouse at Cluny in France was like a large hotel, with seventy-five beds in two separate wings, one for women and one for men.

Monks sing the Psalms, from memory, in the choir of their church. Some of them have fallen asleep.

A Monk's Day

IN THE ELEVENTH CENTURY, a monk's day began between 2 A.M. and 3 A.M., depending on the time of year, when a bell was rung, calling everybody to church. Monks each took their turn to stay awake and ring the bell. They could roughly tell the time by the length of a candle, kept burning throughout the night.

Prayer and Song

The monks slept in their clothes so that they would be ready for prayer. When they heard the bell, they rose from their beds and walked silently to their church, which was lit by flickering candles. Here they sang the first service of the day, called Nocturns (night) or Matins (morning). Nocturns was the longest of all the services, and could last up to two hours. It was often hard to stay awake, and devils were said to lurk in the choir, weighing down the monks' eyelids to make them sleepy. One of the monks walked up and down, carrying a lantern, to make sure that everyone was singing. If he found a sleeping monk, he gently woke him by waving his lantern in front of his face.

In the eleventh century, the Archbishop of Canterbury wrote a book of rules for his monastery. He described how monks who had done wrong should be whipped:

He who is to undergo punishment shall be scourged (whipped) either with a single stout rod ... or with a bundle of finer rods while he sits with a bare back.... While he is being scourged, all the brothers should bow down with a kindly and brotherly compassion (pity) for him.

The Monastic Constitutions of Lanfranc

Monks walk into the church of their monastery to sing the services. The painting shows the seriousness of the monks, who do not look at each other or speak as they follow their religious duties.

In this nineteenth-century painting medieval monks are seen listening to a reading from a religious text as they silently eat their meal in the refectory.

After Nocturns, the monks waited in the choir, praying, until it was time to sing a second service, called Lauds (praise). This was followed at intervals throughout the day by Prime (first), Terce (third), Sext (sixth), and Nones (ninth), named after the hours when they took place. The last two services were Vespers (evening) and Compline (completed).

Work and Mealtimes

In between the services, the monks read, prayed, and worked. In the eleventh century, a monk's work was light, such as weeding the monastery garden or shelling beans.

Each morning, the monks gathered for a meeting in the chapter house, where the abbot discussed the day's business. Monks who had broken any rules confessed and asked to be forgiven. The abbot decided on a punishment, such as having to live on bread and water for a certain time. There was a separate meeting for the boys, where those who had misbehaved or fallen asleep in church were beaten with a bundle of sticks.

In winter, there was just one meal a day, at around 2 P.M. In summer, there were two meals, at midday and in the evening. Meals were eaten in silence, while a monk gave a reading from the Bible or other religious work.

Sign Language

Most of the time, monks were forbidden to speak. This created a peaceful atmosphere, which must have helped them live together. They could not quarrel or gossip about each other. In order to communicate, they had to learn sign language. At meals, a monk asked for fish by moving his hand like a fish swimming through water. Bread was requested by touching thumbs and forefingers together, making a circle, like a round loaf. The sign for a book was to hold the hand out flat and turn it over, like a page.

The Scriptorium

EVERY MONASTERY had a scriptorium, or writing place, where monks copied books and wrote new works by hand. This was found on one side of the cloister, the covered square walkway next to the monastery church. The books produced here included the Bible, lives of the **saints**, and works on medicine, music, and history. History was studied for religious reasons, because great events, such as wars and floods, were believed to show the workings of God.

Writing Tools

Books were written on parchment, the specially prepared skins of sheep, lambs, calves, and goats. Monks did not make the parchment themselves, but bought it from a parchment maker. To prepare the skins, he would soak them in a mixture of lime and water for three days, loosening the hairs. After scraping the hair away with a knife, he stretched the skin over a frame to dry it. There was further scraping of the dried skin, to make the sheets soft and thin.

Our word pen comes from the Latin *penna*, meaning feather. The origin lies in the goose feathers that the monks used to write with. Each monk would make his own pen, cutting and sharpening the nib with a penknife. Black ink was made from galls,

A monk at work in the scriptorium writes on a steep book rest.

Matthew Paris (*c.* 1200–1259) was an English monk at St. Albans who spent thirty-three years writing a chronicle, or year-by-year history of his times, which he decorated with beautiful pictures. This is how he was described by a later monk:

He collected the deeds of great men from ancient times until the end of his own life, writing them down fully in books, together with many marvellous events. Moreover, he was so skilled a workman in gold and silver, in carving and in painting, that he is believed to have left no equal in this world.

Thomas Walsingham, *Deeds of the Abbots, c.* 1420

swellings found on oak trees where a wasp had laid its eggs, or from soot mixed with gum, the dried sticky sap of the acacia tree.

In some of the monks' books, we find descriptions of the work in the scriptorium. A German monk, Ludwig of Wessobrun, wrote: "The book you see was written in the outer seats (of the cloister); while I wrote I froze, and what I could not write by daylight, I finished by candlelight." An unknown English monk wrote: "Three fingers write, yet the whole body is in travail (hard work). Those who do not know how to write do not think it is labour!"

Illuminations

As well as being writers, many medieval monks were skilled artists, who decorated their books with colorful pictures, called illuminations. Nuns were also artists, though they usually specialized in embroidery (needlework), decorating richly colored fabrics for the altars of the church. They also made the vestments, or special robes, worn by priests.

Spectacles

As they grew older, monks often had problems with failing eyesight. They were greatly helped by the invention of spectacles, in Italy in the 1270s. The earliest record of their use dates from 1289, when a man called Sandro di Popozo wrote: "I am so debilitated [weakened] with age that without the glasses known as spectacles, I would no longer be able to read or write." Early spectacles had to be held in one hand or carefully balanced on the nose. Frames with arms were not invented until the eighteenth century.

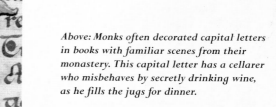

Above: Monks often decorated capital letters in books with familiar scenes from their monastery. This capital letter has a cellarer who misbehaves by secretly drinking wine, as he fills the jugs for dinner.

Left: This capital letter, a Q, contains two monks chopping wood.

Pilgrimage

TRAVEL WAS DIFFICULT and dangerous in the Middle Ages. On country roads, travelers risked being robbed or killed by thieves, and most people were scared of sea crossings. Despite this, every year, hundreds of thousands of men and women left their homes and set off on long journeys to holy places. These journeys were called pilgrimages.

All classes, from kings to peasants, traveled on pilgrimages. While the rich could travel in comfort, the poor had to beg for food and shelter. This was usually freely given, for Christians believed that helping a pilgrim was a holy act, which would be rewarded in heaven.

Paying Penance

The Church taught that a pilgrimage was a penance, an act making amends to God for sins. In 1052–1053, Earl Swein Godwinesson, a powerful English nobleman, walked barefoot all the way to Jerusalem, as penance for murdering his cousin, Beorn. By undergoing such a long and difficult journey, Swein hoped to show God how sorry he was, and to avoid being punished in the next life.

The Power of Relics

The most popular destinations for pilgrimages were the tombs of Christ in Jerusalem, Saint Peter in Rome, and Saint James at Compostela in Spain. There were also many other pilgrimage sites throughout Europe, most of them churches containing **relics**, such as the bones, hair, or the belongings of saints. Relics were thought to have

These pilgrims leaving Canterbury travel in a large group, both for protection and for company on their journey.

Angély, in France, was one of several places claiming to have the head of Saint John the Baptist. A guidebook for pilgrims described the head:

The most holy head is worshipped day and night by a choir of one hundred monks. While this head was being transported on sea and land, it already gave many signs of countless marvels. On sea, it drove away many a danger, and on land … it restored the dead to life. That is the reason why one believes that this is the true head.

Aymeric Picaud, *The Book of Saint James*, c. 1135

special powers, such as the ability to cure the sick. For a medieval pilgrim, coming close to a relic was a way of making a direct link with the saint in heaven. Each year, millions of Catholics still travel on pilgrimages.

For a church or town, owning a famous relic was a source of wealth. Kings and nobles paid for richly decorated **shrines**, where the relics were stored. Pilgrims brought gifts to the church, and paid for souvenirs, such as lead or cloth badges. The most popular pilgrimage in England was to Canterbury Cathedral, where pilgrims could buy little bottles containing the blood, greatly watered down, of Saint Thomas Becket, who had been murdered there in 1170.

Relics on Tour

When a church needed money for some special reason, it might send its relics out on tour. In 1112, for example, the Cathedral of Laon in France burned down. The monks of Laon traveled through the country, carrying the bones of their saint with them in a jeweled shrine, and asking people to contribute money to their rebuilding work.

Relic Thieves

Relics were so valuable that they were often stolen. In 1020, a monk from Jumièges in France went on a pilgrimage to Rome, where he stole the head of Saint Valentine, and took it home to his own monastery. Relic thieves claimed that they were obeying the wishes of the saint. If he had not wanted his head to go to Jumièges, Saint Valentine could easily have prevented its theft.

This is the cloak and purse of Saint John of Capistrano (1386–1456), two relics still carefully preserved in a church in Italy.

Town Life

A MEDIEVAL TOWN was a settlement larger than a village, with a population numbered in thousands rather than hundreds. Unlike villages, towns had the right to govern themselves with a council of the leading burgesses (citizens). Towns could collect taxes and have their own law courts. A town's rights, granted by the king or local lord, were written down in a document called a charter.

The Germans had a saying that town air makes you free. Unlike serfs, townspeople had the freedom to come and go as they pleased and to work solely for themselves. In many places, there was a custom that serfs who ran

Hamburg, Germany, shown in this illustration from its charter, was a thriving medieval town.

New Towns

Between the twelfth and the thirteenth centuries, there was a great rise in the number of towns. Existing towns swelled in size, and hundreds of new ones were founded. In 1180, there were just eight towns beside the Rhine River in Germany. By 1250, there were fifty-two. Kings and lords encouraged the founding of these towns as a way of raising money. The citizens often had to pay their lord for their charter. Lords were also able to charge a sum of money, called a toll, from everybody who sold goods in the town market.

away from the countryside, and were able to spend a year and a day in a town without being recaptured, gained their freedom.

Throughout most of Europe, the larger towns were surrounded by strong walls with heavy gates, which were locked at night. The main purpose was protection from attack. The walls also served to mark off the town as a separate place, with its own laws and rights.

Buildings

Inside the town walls, space for building was scarce. To make the most use of the land available, people built upward, so that houses had two and sometimes three floors. The upper floors also jutted out over the lower ones, providing even more room. This meant that houses were often close together, cutting out light from the street below.

A medieval town, packed with buildings and surrounded by high walls, from a fifteenth-century wall painting in Florence, Italy.

Dirt and Disease

Medieval towns were often filthy and smelly places. Anyone walking down the streets had to take care to avoid the dung dropped by animals, the garbage thrown out of the upper windows of the houses, and the rotting fish and meat dumped by the fishmongers and butchers.

In most towns, there were no sewers to take away waste from toilets, which were usually just holes dug in the backyards behind the houses. These cesspits had to be regularly emptied onto carts, whose contents were emptied in the local river or spread on fields outside the town. In hot summers, town cesspits swarmed with flies.

Because people lived in large numbers closely together, often in filthy conditions, diseases spread very quickly. Death rates in medieval towns were always higher than birth rates. Even so, the population of towns continued to rise, thanks to the constant arrival of newcomers from the countryside.

Fires

With tightly packed wooden buildings, the greatest risk of town life was from fire. When a fire broke out, it would quickly spread, and nothing could be done to stop it. Between 1077 and 1227, there were nine major fires in London, destroying large areas of the city. In many towns, a bell was rung at nightfall, warning people to cover or put out their fires. This was called the curfew, from the French *couvre-feu* (cover fire).

Markets and Fairs

ONCE A WEEK, a market was held in a square in the middle of a town, where goods were displayed on stalls. The peasants from the countryside brought their crops and animals to the market, and the **craftworkers** and **merchants** of the town could also sell their goods there.

Churchmen sometimes complained about the bad language heard on market day, as people argued over prices. Around 1270, a French friar, Humbert of Romans, wrote: "You will hear men swearing there: 'By God I will not give you so much for it…,' or 'By God I will not take a smaller price…,' or 'By God it is not worth so much as that….'"

In the big cities, such as Paris and London, several different markets were held in one week, each selling different types of goods. From the twelfth century, a famous sight of London was the weekly horse market, which took place just to the north of the city walls, at Smithfield.

A Londoner called William FitzStephen described the races held at the weekly horse market at Smithfield:

When a race is about to begin … a shout is raised…. Jockeys who mount these flying steeds … prepare themselves…. Their mounts also enter into the spirit of the contest…. When the signal is given, they stretch their limbs to the uttermost, and dash down the course with courageous speed. The riders … plunge their spurs into the horses and urge them forward with shouts and whips.

William FitzStephen, *Life of Thomas Becket*, 1170s

A busy cloth market, in Bologna, Italy, with a man in the center who appears to have been caught stealing.

Punishments

It was on market day that people were punished for wrongdoing. Thieves might be hanged, branded with a hot iron, or have a hand or ear chopped off. The punishment depended on whether it was a first offense, and on the value of the goods stolen. All medieval people were used to the sight of blood being shed, and many of them enjoyed it.

Punishments for minor offenses were designed to shame, or make people look foolish in front of their neighbors. A man caught selling rotten meat would be forced to sit for the whole of market day locked in a wooden frame, called a pillory, while the townsfolk pelted him with garbage.

Fairs

Two or three times a year, towns held great fairs, often in a field outside the town walls. Merchants from far and wide traveled to fairs, so many more goods were available than at the weekly market. Fairs also attracted traveling entertainers, such as musicians, jugglers, tumblers (acrobats), tightrope walkers, fire-eaters, and men with performing bears, horses, and dogs. In most towns, the fair, which might last for two weeks, was the most exciting event of the year.

In October 1248, Henry III of England (1216–1272) decided to hold a new fair in Westminster. According to an English monk, it was ruined by bad weather:

Those who showed their goods for sale there suffered great inconvenience because of the lack of roofs apart from canvas awnings.... Gusts of wind, usual at that time of year, battered the merchants so that they were cold and wet.... Their feet were dirtied by the mud and their merchandise spoilt by the rain.

Matthew Paris, *Great Chronicle, c.* 1250

Guilds

MOST MEDIEVAL CRAFTS and trades were controlled by organizations called **guilds**. Guilds, such as those of carpenters, glassmakers, and wool merchants, made sure that goods on sale were of a proper standard, and prevented people who were not guild members from trading in the town. They also set wages and prices, so that nobody could sell goods cheaper than their neighbors. Unlike modern businesses, which compete with one another, the guild system was based on cooperation: people worked together, so that all the members were able to make a living. Guilds also cared for their members in times of hardship and sickness.

Apprentices, Journeymen, and Masters

Entry into a guild was through **apprenticeship**. A guild member who had his own business, called a master, took a boy apprentice (learner) into his household. The apprentice would serve the master for several years, in return for being fed, clothed, and taught his craft. At the end of his apprenticeship, his work would be examined by the senior guild members. If it was good enough, he became a journeyman, or worker paid by the day (*journée* in French).

Journeymen who worked hard could one day set up their own businesses and become masters. First they had to pass a test, producing a piece of work, such as a chair, a sword, or a painting, which was called their masterpiece.

This painting from 1380 is taken from a book which belonged to a guild of Italian wool merchants.

Mystery plays are still performed today, staged on carts, as they were in the Middle Ages.

Mystery Plays

In 1264, the Church introduced a new religious festival, called Corpus Christi (Christ's body), which took place in early June. In the fourteenth century, it became the custom for British guilds in large towns to put on religious plays during the festival. These were called mystery plays, after *mystery*, another name for a craft. The plays formed a cycle, or series, telling the whole story of the Bible from the creation of the world.

Each guild performed its play on top of a richly decorated cart called a pageant. There was a great deal of rivalry between the richer guilds, which spent large sums of money on carts, costumes, and scenery. Preparation and rehearsal went on for weeks. People came from miles around to see the plays, so all the guild members wanted to put on a wonderful show, to demonstrate their pride in their guild and in their town.

At the start of the Chester Mystery Plays, verses were read out listing the coming attractions. One was the colorful pageant cart of the Mercers, or sellers of fine cloth:

It shall be decked, that all the rowte [people]
Full gladly on it shall be to look;
With sundry [several] colours it shall shine
Of velvet, satin and damask fine
Taffeta sersnet [shining silk] of popinjay [parrot] green.

Banns of the Chester Plays, c. 1467

33

The Hanseatic League

IN THE THIRTEENTH CENTURY, the towns of Hamburg and Lübeck in northern Germany had close trading links with each other. Lübeck, on the coast of the Baltic Sea, drew its wealth from herring, caught in vast numbers in waters south of Sweden. Hamburg, which lies inland, was a supplier of good quality salt, dug out of the earth in mines. Working together, these towns created a new product, salted herring, which could be sold all over northern Europe. This was in great demand because of all the fish days when the Church banned the eating of meat.

Hamburg and Lübeck both lie near the borders of Denmark, a powerful kingdom which was seen as a threat. In 1241, the two towns made a treaty, or agreement, to help each other if either were attacked, and to promote their own trades. Soon other German towns joined this grouping, which came to be called the Hanseatic League, or Hansa, a German word meaning company. At its height, in the late fourteenth century, almost two hundred German towns were members of the league.

Squirrel Furs

In winter, the northern squirrel of Scandinavia and Russia grows a beautiful thick blue-gray coat. This fur was highly prized in western Europe, where it was used to line robes and to decorate clothing worn by the rich. The demand was so great that the rulers of Novgorod in Russia made their peasants pay taxes in squirrel skins, which they then sold to the Hanseatic merchants. Records show that over a twelve-month period, in 1390–1391, the Germans brought 350,960 squirrel skins to London.

The wealth of medieval Lübeck can be seen from the number of big churches with tall towers.

Trading Posts

The league set up trading posts, called *kontors*, in London, Novgorod in Russia, Bruges in Flanders (modern Belgium), and Bergen in Norway. The London *kontor*, called the Steelyard, lay beside the Thames River, and included warehouses, offices, and living quarters. Here the Easterlings, as the English called the Germans, sold timber and **stockfish** (dried cod) from Norway, furs and beeswax from Russia, cloth from Flanders, flax and hemp from the eastern Baltic, and their own salted herring. They bought English wool, which they shipped abroad to sell.

The main aim of the league was to have sole right of buying and selling. So, although they set up *kontors* in other countries, they refused to let foreign merchants have bases in their own towns, or in Novgorod and Bergen. Almost all the goods traded between Norway, Russia, and England were carried in Hanseatic ships.

The Hansa obtained special rights not given to other merchants, such as freedom from paying tolls. Foreign rulers agreed to these conditions because there was such a great demand for the Hansa's goods. If England had refused to trade with the league, the country would have lost its main source of cheap fish.

This model of a Hanseatic cog shows its high sides, which allowed it to carry large cargoes and also helped to protect the ship from attack.

The Cog

The Hanseatic League carried its goods in a new type of merchant ship called a cog. It had a bigger belly than other ships of the time, which meant that it could carry more goods. Unlike earlier ships, steered using an oar on one side of the ship, the cog had a large rudder fixed at the stern (rear). Stern rudders were bigger and stronger than steering oars, and also easier to use. The league owned hundreds of cogs, which crossed the North Sea and the Baltic in fleets, for protection against attack.

Famine and Plague

IN THE EARLY 1300s, the climate of Europe cooled. Summers grew shorter, cooler, and wetter, while the winters were bitterly cold. In 1303–1304 and 1306–1307 it was so cold that the Baltic Sea froze, trapping the Hanseatic cogs in their harbors.

In 1315 and 1316, two wet summers in a row led to harvest failures, and also spread animal diseases, killing vast numbers of sheep and cattle. Peasants grew so hungry that they ate the oxen that pulled their plows, and the seeds they had saved for planting. The result was a terrible famine, which affected most of northern Europe. Stories were told of men and women eating their own children, and of the old starving themselves to death to give the young a better chance to survive. In some German towns, soldiers were sent to guard the gallows, to stop people from cutting down the bodies of executed criminals and eating them. By 1317, even the rich were going hungry.

An English monk described the wet summers of 1315 and 1316:

The hand of God was raised against us.... In the previous year there was such heavy rain that men could scarcely harvest the corn or bring it safely to the barn. In the present year worse happened. Floods of rain rotted almost all the seed.... In many places the hay lay so long under water that it could be neither mown nor gathered. Sheep everywhere died and other animals were killed by a sudden plague.

Written by an unknown monk, *Life of Edward II, c.* 1325

During famine years, beggars, like these men receiving gifts of food, were the first to starve to death. Several here are disabled.

Weeping and praying, the people of Perugia in Italy flee their plague-stricken city.

The Black Death

Population levels slowly recovered from the famine, only for Europe to be hit by a deadly disease called the Black Death. This disease, now thought to be **bubonic plague**, first appeared in China in the late 1320s, and then spread west, along trade routes. It was carried by the fleas of rats, which swarmed in the holds of the merchant ships.

In 1347, the plague reached European ports, such as Messina in Sicily and Genoa in Italy. Hundreds of people died each day, and those who were still healthy fled to other cities, taking the disease with them. The plague spread everywhere, striking even remote monasteries. Thousands of villages were deserted. According to one Italian, "Father abandoned child, wife husband, one brother another, for this illness seemed to strike through breath and sight…. None could be found to bury the dead for money or friendship."

Nobody knew the true cause of the disease, which was widely believed to be a punishment sent by God for their sins. In Germany people went on religious processions, weeping, praying, and lashing themselves with whips, in an attempt to fend off God's anger.

By 1352, 25 million people had died from the plague—one out of every three people in Europe.

A citizen of Siena in Italy described the plague in his own city:

Great pits were dug and piled deep with the … dead. And they died by the hundreds both day and night, and all were thrown in those ditches…. And as soon as those ditches were filled more were dug. And I, Agnolo di Tura, called the Fat, buried my five children with my own hands…. There was no one who wept for any death, for all awaited death. And so many died that all believed that it was the end of the world.

Agnolo di Tura, *Great Chronicle*

Peasants' Uprisings

THE BLACK DEATH created a big labor shortage. There were fewer peasants to do the work, and they felt they deserved better conditions. Serfs began to demand their freedom, while free peasants who were paid wages wanted more. However, the labor shortage also meant that the great landholders had lost much of their income from their land. They did not want to give in to the peasants' demands. Kings made laws to try to keep wages low and stop peasants from moving freely about the country.

The Jacquerie

From 1337, England and France were at war. This war was unpopular in France because the French knights lost every battle they fought. The greatest disaster was the Battle of Poitiers, in 1356, when the French king was taken prisoner along with many of his leading nobles. French nobles were no longer able to protect their own peasants from raiding by English armies.

In the spring of 1358, discontent with the nobility led to a great uprising by the French

Jean de Froissart, a French writer, describes the French peasants' uprising:

They declared that the nobles ... were bringing the kingdom to shame and destruction and that it would be a good idea to destroy them all.... Wherever they went, their numbers increased, for everyone who shared their opinion joined them. Knights and squires, nobles and girls fled wherever they could ... abandoning their manors and castles.

Jean de Froissart, *Chronicle*, 1370s

A group of knights kills rebellious French peasants during the Jacquerie uprising.

In 1381, the English rebel leader, Wat Tyler, is killed by the mayor of London in front of the king, who is also shown calming the rebels after the killing.

peasants. This was known as the Jacquerie, from Jacques, a common peasant name. In the region around Paris, peasants attacked castles, and killed every knight and lady they could get hold of. The Jacquerie was eventually crushed by King Charles II of Navarre in Spain (1387–1425), who was worried about rebellion spreading to his own kingdom.

Peasants' Revolt

To pay for the war against France, in 1380 the English government brought in a new tax. This was hated by the peasants because it was a **poll tax**—a tax on individuals, who all had to pay the same amount, no matter how rich or poor they were.

In June 1381, the peasants in Kent and Essex attacked the tax collectors. In each county, they gathered in large numbers and marched on London. King Richard II (1377–1399), fourteen years old at the time, had two meetings with the rebels outside London, where he agreed to all their demands and promised to free the serfs. The peasants trusted the young king, but once they had gone home, he broke his word. The leaders of the uprising were hunted down and hanged.

Although these peasants' rebellions failed, governments could not stop the peasants from demanding and receiving better conditions. Laws designed to keep wages low and stop peasants from leaving their villages were simply ignored. In time, serfdom gradually disappeared.

One of the leaders of the English peasants' revolt was a priest called John Ball. According to Jean de Froissart, Ball traveled around the country preaching that everybody should be equal:

Things cannot go well in England until everything is owned by all the people together, and there is no difference between gentlefolk and peasants. We all come from the same father and mother, Adam and Eve. How then can they say that they are greater than us, except by making us work to produce the wealth they spend?

Jean de Froissart, *Chronicle*, 1390s

The Cities of Italy

WHILE THE HANSEATIC LEAGUE handled much of the trade of northern Europe (see pages 34–35), in the south the merchants of northern Italy were also growing rich and powerful, selling spices and other **luxury goods**. The leading Italian merchant cities were Florence, Genoa, Venice, Pisa, Milan, and Siena.

In theory, northern Italy was part of the vast **Holy Roman Empire**, which stretched across Europe. In reality, the emperor had little power in Italy, and each Italian city was like a small state, ruling both itself and the surrounding countryside. City-state governments, known as communes, made their own laws and had their own armies. Unlike the German towns, they never united in a league, for they were bitter rivals. Florence was often at war with Pisa, Milan, or Siena, while the Genoese frequently fought the Venetians.

Florence

Florence means flourishing town, a name well suited to this Italian city. From the thirteenth century, the city grew rich selling silks and jewelry. The Florentines also set up some of Europe's first banks, where people could deposit their own money for safekeeping, and also borrow. The bankers made money by charging interest—an extra amount paid back in

Usury

To the Church, charging interest on a loan, as the Italian bankers did, was a sin, called usury. This meant that the Church banned the practice. Yet the services of bankers were so useful that people found ways around this ban. When drawing up **contracts**, bankers often disguised the interest sum as another sort of payment, such as a fine for late repayment of the loan.

By studying ancient Roman buildings, fifteenth-century Italian architects learned how to build great domes, like this one on the Cathedral in Florence, built by Brunelleschi between 1420 and 1446.

addition to the original loan. The monies deposited were also invested in various business ventures.

The most famous Florentine bank was set up by Giovanni de Medici in 1397. Medici established branches throughout Italy, and in France, Bruges, and London. When European kings needed to raise money in a hurry, they often went to the Medici bank.

The Medicis became so influential that in 1434, Cosimo (1389–1476), son of Giovanni, was able to take power in Florence. During his rule, which lasted over thirty years, Cosimo spent vast sums as a patron (supporter) of the arts. He hired the finest artists, such as the sculptor Donatello (1386–1466), who made a bronze bust of Cosimo's wife, and the architect and sculptor Filippo Brunelleschi (1377–1446), who built churches for him. Cosimo also employed scholars to translate the writings of ancient Greeks into Latin, and opened the first public library in Europe.

Cosimo de Medici was just one of many fifteenth-century Italian patrons of the arts. They used their wealth to bring about a rediscovery of ancient Greek and ancient Roman learning and art. Today, we call this period the Renaissance (which means rebirth in French).

The Florentine Giovanni Villani described the food supply of his city:

It has been estimated that there are in Florence upwards of 90,000 mouths, including men, women and children, from the evidence of the bread which is continuously needed in the city.... The city required every year about 400 cows and calves, 60,000 sheep, 20,000 goats and 30,000 pigs. In the month of July through the gate of San Frediano, there came 4,000 loads of melons which were distributed throughout the city.

Giovanni Villani, *Florentine Chronicle, c.* 1338

New Books

IN THE EARLY MIDDLE AGES, almost all European books were produced by monks. Then, in the 1200s, the first universities were set up, teaching medicine, law, and religion to students. Universities needed more books than the monks could produce, so they employed professional book copiers called scribes, who set up workshops in cities like Paris and London.

The demand for books increased in the fourteenth century. The growing class of merchants had to read and write for their work, and they wanted books for entertainment and instruction, too. They turned to the city scribes, whose workshops grew in size. By the fifteenth century, there were several thousand scribes working in Paris alone, producing copy after copy of the same book. Apart from religious works, they made copies of romances (tales of love and adventure), history books, law books, poems, and travel writings.

A reconstruction of an early printing press, with its great screw, turned by the handle to push the inky letters down onto the paper.

Printing

In the 1420s, people began to print books using wooden blocks. A page of a book would be carved, letter by letter, on a wooden block, which was spread with ink and pressed onto a sheet of

In the fifteenth century, one of the best-selling books across Europe was *The Travels of Sir John Mandeville*. It was written by an English knight who claimed to have traveled throughout Asia and seen many strange marvels:

There is still another isle where the people have only one foot, which is so broad that it will cover all the body and shade it from the sun. They will run so fast on this one foot that it is a marvel to see them.

Sir John Mandeville, *The Travels of Sir John Mandeville, c.* 1356

paper. It took a long time to carve the original block, but it could then be used many times.

In the 1440s, a German goldsmith called Johannes Gutenberg (*c.* 1398–1468) developed a new way of printing, using separate metal letters, slotted into rows to make a page. He also had to invent a new type of oil-based ink, which would stick to metal and transfer clearly onto paper. To print, Gutenberg built a press, similar to the machines already used in papermaking, which was turned to push the letters onto the paper. After years developing his press, in about 1456 Gutenberg printed his first book, a Latin copy of the Bible. It had beautiful clear letters, which were sharper than any that could be carved from wood, and it took much less time to print.

The idea of printing spread rapidly, and by 1480, there were 380 presses across Europe. In the fifty years after Gutenberg's Bible, around 10 million books were printed, far more than all the monks and scribes of the Middle Ages had been able to write by hand.

Paper

In the 1270s, the Italians learned to make paper, a Chinese invention. The paper was made from rotting linen rags which were soaked and mashed into a pulp in a mill. The wet pulp was then placed in a screw press, a machine with a great screw, turned by a lever, which pressed the pulp flat and drove the water out. The sheets of paper were then hung from ropes to dry. Although not as strong as parchment (see page 24), paper was much cheaper. Mass-produced Italian paper was soon sold all over Europe.

Gutenberg made every effort to make his Bible look as beautiful as those hand painted by monks.

The End of the Middle Ages

PRINTING CHANGED EVERYBODY'S LIVES. The Church lost influence, for many townspeople were now better educated than their priests. Ordinary people could read the Bible for themselves, and make up their own minds about what to believe. Those who criticized the Church could also spread their ideas in print. In the 1550s, an Englishman called John Foxe wrote: "Through printing, the world begins now to have eyes to see and hearts to judge."

Age of Exploration

Christopher Columbus (1451–1506) was one man whose life was changed by books. The son of a weaver from Genoa, Italy, Columbus went to sea at an early age, sailing on merchant voyages around the Mediterranean. One of the books he owned was *Imago Mundi (Picture of the World)*, a work of geography written in 1410 by Pierre D'Ailly, a French cardinal. Here D'Ailly argued that it was possible to reach Asia by sailing west from Europe, across the Atlantic Ocean. D'Ailly wrote,

New Fishing Grounds

Off Newfoundland, John Cabot found seas swarming with so many cod that they could be pulled up in bucketloads. The English, soon followed by the French, the Spanish, and the Portuguese, could now catch their own cod rather than buying it from the Hanseatic League. This was a big blow to the Germans, whose trade had been falling off since the 1420s, when the herrings stopped spawning (breeding) in the Baltic. The herrings moved out into the North Sea, where the Dutch could catch them.

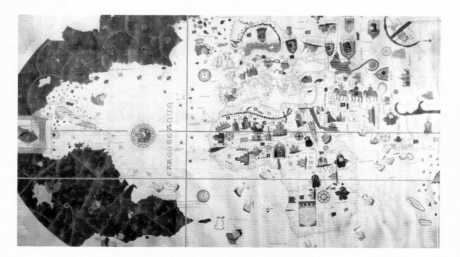

This map, from 1500, is one of the first to show part of America, on the left. At the top, Europe, which had filled most medieval world maps, now looks tiny.

In the sixteenth century, European ships, like the Portuguese fleet shown here, sailed all the world's oceans.

"Between the end of Spain and the beginning of India lies a narrow sea that can be sailed in a few days with a favourable wind."

In 1492, Columbus put D'Ailly's idea to the test, sailing across the Atlantic on behalf of the king and queen of Spain. He reached the islands of the Caribbean, and began the discovery of a new continent, America, whose existence had not even been suspected before by Europeans.

Other people were reading the same books as Columbus and coming up with the same ideas. In 1497, John Cabot (*c.* 1451–1498), a Venetian, made an Atlantic crossing on behalf of the king of England, and reached Newfoundland. In 1498, the Portuguese explorer Vasco da Gama (*c.* 1469–1525) set off on a voyage which would take him around Africa all the way to India and back.

As a result of these voyages, Europeans learned about the wider world. This was the beginning of a new age, the Age of Exploration.

Modern History

For convenience, historians use the year 1500 to mark the end of the Middle Ages and the start of modern history. Yet most people living at the time had little sense that they were moving from one age to another. Across Europe, monks still got up in the middle of the night to sing Matins, peasants still rose at dawn to yoke their oxen to plows, and nobles flew their peregrine falcons, as they had done for centuries past.

Vasco da Gama

Vasco da Gama's 1497–1499 voyage to India and back opened up a new route for the spices of Asia. Portugal, previously one of the poorest countries in Europe, would now grow rich on cheap spices. This was a disaster for the cities of northern Italy and the merchants they traded with. A business report from Ravensburg, Germany, recorded, "There is no demand for spices whatever, since everyone is expecting news from Portugal."

Chronology

1000	Leif Eriksson, a Viking explorer, reaches North America.
1066	Normans conquer England.
c. 1150	Silk production begins in Sicily.
c. 1180	Compass in use in Europe; rudders are used for the first time on ships in northern Europe.
1185	Earliest record of a windmill in England.
c. 1200	University of Paris founded.
1200s	The spinning wheel, probably an Indian invention, reaches Europe.
1202	Arabic numbers (1, 2, 3, 4, etc.) first used in Europe.
1212	Thatched roofs in London start to be replaced with tiles.
c. 1235	Buttons first used on clothes, in Germany.
1241	Hamburg and Lübeck sign a treaty, which will lead to the formation of the Hanseatic League.
1264	Introduction of the Festival of Corpus Christi.
c. 1270	Papermaking begins in Italy.
c. 1280	Earliest known European sea chart, the *Carte Pisano*.
1289	Earliest record of reading glasses in Italy.
c. 1310	First mechanical clocks built.
1315–1317	A series of cold, wet summers causes famine across northern Europe.
1332	Oranges first go on sale in Europe.
1337	Beginning of Hundred Years' War between France and England.
1347–1352	Black Death spreads through Europe.
1358	Peasants' uprising in France, known as the Jacquerie.
1381	The Peasants' Revolt in England.
1419	Portuguese begin to send out ships to explore the African coast and the Atlantic.
1420–1446	Filippo Brunelleschi builds the dome of the Cathedral in Florence.
1420s	Herring move their breeding grounds from the Baltic to the North Sea.
1441	Portuguese bring first African slaves to Lisbon.
c. 1456	Johannes Gutenberg prints his first book, a Bible.
1492	The Italian explorer Christopher Columbus sails across the Atlantic and reaches the Caribbean.
1497–1499	The Portuguese explorer Vasco da Gama sails around Africa to India.
1498	The Italian explorer John Cabot sails across the Atlantic and discovers the Newfoundland cod-fishing banks.

For Further Research

Books

Peter Chrisp, *The Medieval Church*. London: Hodder Wayland, 1996.

Christopher Gravett, *DK Eyewitness Guide: Castle*. London: Dorling Kindersley, 2000.

Christopher Gravett, *DK Eyewitness Guide: Knight*. London: Dorling Kindersley, 2000.

Christopher Gravett, *The World of the Medieval Knight*. London: Hodder Wayland, 2001.

Fiona McDonald and Mark Bergin, *A Medieval Castle*. New York: Peter Bedrick Books, 1993.

Paul B. Newman, *Daily Life in the Middle Ages*. Jefferson, North Carolina, and London: McFarland, 2001.

Sources

J.A. Barrow, ed., *Sir Gawain and the Green Knight*. Harmondsworth, UK: Penguin, 1972.

William Bowsky, ed., *Black Death a Turning Point in History?* Austin, TX: Holt, Rinehart and Winston, 1971.

Geoffrey Brereton, trans., *Froissart Chronicles*. Harmondsworth, UK: Penguin Classics, 1968.

G.G. Coulton, *Medieval Village*. Cambridge, UK: Cambridge University Press, 1925.

G.G. Coulton, *Social Life in Britain from the Conquest to the Reformation*. Cambridge, UK: Cambridge University Press, 1918.

John Cummins, *The Hound and the Hawk: The Art of Medieval Hunting*. London: Phoenix Press, 2001.

Piers the Ploughman by William Langland, translated by J.F. Goodridge. Harmondsworth, UK: Penguin Classics, 1966.

Elizabeth Hallam, ed., *Chronicles of the Age of Chivalry*. London: Guild, 1989.

David Herlihy, ed., *Medieval Culture and Society*. London: Macmillan, 1968.

David Knowles, trans., *Monastic Constitutions of Lanfranc*. London: Thomas Nelson and Sons, 1951.

C.W.R.D. Moseley, trans., *The Travels of Sir John Mandeville*. Harmondsworth, UK: Penguin Classics, 1983.

Michael Swanton, trans., *Anglo-Saxon Prose*. London: J.M. Dent Everyman, 1993.

Glossary

apprenticeship A system of learning a trade, in which a boy is bound, or made to serve a master, for a set period.

bailiffs Manor officials, paid by a lord to collect his rents.

bless To bring God's favor onto something, whether a person, an animal, or an action. Priests are believed to have the power to bless.

bubonic plague A deadly disease. Symptoms include large swellings in the armpits and groin, called buboes.

chamberlain The official in charge of running the household of a king or rich noble.

Communion Ceremony in which holy bread and wine, believed to be changed by a priest into Christ's body and blood, are eaten and drunk.

confession Owning up to faults or wrongdoing. Christians confess their sins to a priest so that they will be worthy to receive Communion.

contracts Written business agreements.

craftworkers Workers skilled at making things, such as furniture, pottery, or jewelry.

curse The opposite of bless—to bring God's disfavor onto something.

demesne The home farm, the part of a manor kept by the lord of the manor for his own use.

Domesday Book Name given to the survey of England undertaken in 1086–1087 for William the Conqueror. Domesday means day of judgment.

dowry Property or money brought by a bride to her husband on marriage.

fallow Land that is left unplanted with crops.

fast days Days when the Church orders people to fast, or give up certain foods.

furrow Long groove made in the earth by a plow.

guilds Craft or trade organizations, found in most medieval towns.

hand mills Devices for grinding grain into flour by hand. Often they take the form of two circular flat stones, the upper one with a central hole. A wooden handle is used to turn the upper stone, while grain is dropped into the hole.

Holy Roman Empire The medieval empire in western Europe that included Germany, a small part of France, and much of Italy.

knights Noble warriors who usually fought on horseback, wearing expensive armor.

luxury goods Goods which are costly and not essential for life, such as spices and silk cloth.

Mass A church service during which medieval Christians believed bread and wine were changed into the body and blood of Christ.

men-at-arms Knights and commoners armed as knights (called sergeants).

merchants People who live by buying and selling.

peasant A poor farmer. The word comes from the French *paysan*, meaning country dweller.

poll tax A tax on individual people, rather than on land or property. Poll means head.

purgatory A place of suffering, where the dead have their sins burned away, so that they are worthy to go to heaven to be with God. Most medieval Christians believed that they would have to spend many years in purgatory. Purgatory means making pure.

reeve Manor official in charge of the day-to-day farmwork.

relics Any holy objects belonging to or linked with a saint, such as items of clothing or bones.

saints Holy people believed by Christians to have special powers, given by God. In the Middle Ages, for example, Christians believed that many saints had the power to cure illnesses.

serf Semi-free peasant forced to work for a lord in return for the right to grow his own food.

shrine A container for a relic, which might be a small jeweled box, for a piece of wood from Christ's cross, or a large stone tomb, for a saint's body.

sins Actions or thoughts that Christians believe displease God.

slaves People bought and sold and treated as property. Slaves have no rights.

steward The senior official paid by a lord to oversee the running of his estates.

stockfish Dried fish, mostly cod, from Norway, so called because it was hung out to dry on racks made from *stokks* (sticks).

sundial An instrument for measuring the time of day. It has a metal rod, called a gnomon, which casts a shadow on a dial, showing the movement of the sun.

tithe A tax levied on peasants, which was given to the Church. Tithe means tenth and the tax was one-tenth of a person's income.

villeins A name for serfs used in the *Domesday Book*, from Latin villa (farm). It later gave rise to the word villain—someone with a bad character.

Index

Figures in **bold** *refer to pictures.*
All monarchs are English, unless
otherwise stated.

apprentices 32

bailiffs 8, 9, 15
banking 40, 41, **41**
Black Death, the 5, 37, **37**
books 24, 25, 42, 43, **43**

Cabot, John 45
childbirth 14
children 10, 14, 17
Christianity 12, 13
Church, the 4, 18, 26, 33, 34, 44
churches 12, 13, **13**, 25, 27
cities 30, 40, 41
clocks 5
Columbus, Christopher 44, 45
cooking 18, 19, **19**
countryside 4
craftworkers 4, 30

death 12
demesne 7, 8
disease 29
Domesday Book, the 6, 7

entertainment 31

fairs 31
famine 36, **36**
farmers 4, 7, **7**, 8, **8**
farming 5, **7**, 8, **8**, 9, **9**, 10, **10**, 11, **11**
feasts **18**, 19
fire 29

food 5, 16, 18, 19, **19**, 21

guilds 32, **32**, 33
Gutenberg, Johannes 43

Hanseatic cogs 35, **35**
Hanseatic League 34, 35
houses 29
hunting 16, **16**, 17, **17**

illuminations 25, **25**

journeymen 32
jousting 15, **15**

kings 6, 16, 17, 21, 26, 28
    Charles II of Navarre 39
    Richard II of England 19, 39
    William the Conqueror 6, 7, 16
knights 6, 14, 15, **15**

lighting 5

manors 6, 7, 8
maps 44, **44**
markets 30, **30**, 31
marriage 14
Mass 12, 13, 15
merchants 4, 5, 19, 30, 32, 35, 42
midwives **14**
mills 8
monasteries 20, 21
monks 20, 21, **21**, 22, **22**, 23, **23**, 24,
    24, 25, **25**, 27
mystery plays 33, **33**

nobles 4, 6, 14, 15, 16, 17, 18, **18**

Normans, the 6, 7
nuns 20, **20**, 21, 25

peasants 4, 7, 8, **8**, **9**, 10, **10**, 12, 13,
    14, 18, 21, 26, 30, 36, 38, 39, 45
peasants' uprisings
    Jacquerie, the (France) 38, **38**, 39
    Peasants' Revolt, the (England) 39,
        39
pilgrimages 26, **26**, 27
population 5
priests 12, 13, **13**, 25
printing 42, 43, 44
punishments 7, 31, **31**
purgatory 12

reeves 8, 9, **9**
relics 26, 27, **27**
religion 5, 12, 13

serfs 7, 8, 9, **9**, 28
servants 14, 17, 19
slaves 7
spices 19

taxation 7, 28
tithe 12
tournaments 15, **15**
towns 4, **4**, 5, 27, 28, **28**, 29, **29**,
    34
trade 30, 32, 34, 35

villages 6, 9, 12, 28, 37
villeins 7

women 11, 14, 17
writing 24, 25, **25**